Attracting Mates

Kimberley Jane Pryor

Smart Apple Media
P.O. Box 3263
Mankato, MN, 56002

First published in 2010 by
MACMILLAN EDUCATION AUSTRALIA PTY LTD
15–19 Claremont St, South Yarra, Australia 3141

Visit our web site at www.macmillan.com.au or go directly to www.macmillanlibrary.com.au

Associated companies and representatives throughout the world.

Library of Congress Cataloging-in-Publication Data

Pryor, Kimberley Jane.
  Attracting mates / by Kimberley Jane Pryor.
    p. cm. — (Animal lives)
  Includes index.
  Summary: "Gives information on ways animals find their mates and highlights different animals, both large and small from land to sea"—Provided by publisher.
  ISBN 978-1-59920-401-7 (library binding)
  1. Courtship in animals. 2. Mate selection. I. Title.
  QL761.P75 2012
591.56'2—dc22
                                    2010046003

Publisher: Carmel Heron
Managing Editor: Vanessa Lanaway
Editor: Paige Amor and Georgina Garner
Proofreader: Tim Clarke
Designer: Ben Galpin
Page layout: Ben Galpin
Photo researcher: Lesya Bryndzia (management: Debbie Gallagher)
Illustrator: Ben Spiby
Production Controller: Vanessa Johnson

Manufactured in the United States of America by Corporate Graphics
North Mankato, Minnesota
April 2011

Acknowledgements

The author and the publisher are grateful to the following for permission to reproduce copyright material:

Front cover photograph of southern elephant seals, courtesy of Shutterstock/bierchen.

Frank Park/ANTPhoto, **14**; Silvestris Fotoservice/ANTPhoto, **27**, **29**; Dave Watts/ANTPhoto, **24**; Norbert Wu/ANTPhoto, **30**; Kevin Schafer/Corbis, **20**; Norbert Rosing/National Geographic/Getty Images, **19**; iStockphoto.com/Rob Broek, **12**; iStockphoto.com/Jose Tejo, **10**; iStockphoto.com/walkingmoon, **11**; iStockphoto.com/Roger Whiteway, **15**; JupiterImages Unlimited/Photos.com, **8**; Nature Picture Library/Premaphotos, **26**; Photolibrary/Photo Researchers/A Rider, **17**; Photolibrary/Picture Press/Jürgen & Christine Sohns, **9**; Photolibrary/Oxford Scientific (OSF)/Peter Lewis, **22**; Photolibrary/Oxford Scientific (OSF)/Konrad Wothe, **25**; Shutterstock/bierchen, **28**; Shutterstock/Bob Blanchard, **5**; Shutterstock/LaDonna Brezik, **23**; Shutterstock/EcoPrint, **16**; Shutterstock/Kirsanov, **18**; Shutterstock/Anita Patterson Peppers, **13**; Shutterstock/WizData, inc, **21**; Shutterstock/Paul S. Wolf, **4**.

For Nick, Thomas and Ashley

Contents

Animal Lives 4

Attracting Mates 5

Flow Chart: Courtship Display 6
Some birds perform courtship displays on shared breeding grounds, known as leks.

Displaying Tail Feathers 8
Some birds display their spectacular tail feathers to attract mates.

Showing a Color 10
Eye-catching colors can help animals win a mate.

Flashing Colors and Lights 12
Some animals flash bright colors or lights to get noticed.

Singing and Roaring 14
Animals singing sweetly or roaring loudly can get the attention of mates.

Calling 16
Some small animals make surprisingly loud mating calls.

Releasing Smells 18
Some female animals release smells to attract males from a distance.

Dancing 20
Dancing and prancing animals can impress a mate.

Flying 22
Some animals dazzle future mates with their flying skills.

Building Bowers 24
The building and decorating skills of some birds impress future mates.

Giving Gifts 26
Giving gifts protects a male animal or shows that he can find food for young.

Fighting 28
Some male animals fight to show females how strong they are.

Believe It or Not: Staying Together 30

Glossary 31

Index 32

Glossary Words

When a word is printed in **bold**, you can look up its meaning in the glossary on page 31.

Animals face many challenges in their lives. From the moment they are old enough to look after themselves, they have to work hard to survive. They must search for food. They need to escape from hungry **predators**. They have to find or make safe homes so they can shelter from the weather and hide from danger.

When they become adults, animals must attract mates so they can have young. Some animals travel to faraway **breeding** grounds to have their young. After they hatch or are born, many young need to be protected and cared for until they, too, are old enough to survive on their own.

One of the challenges that a male American alligator faces is to attact a mate. He does this by raising his head out of the water and bellowing.

Attracting Mates

Most adult animals need to attract mates to have young. An animal sometimes behaves in a certain way to make itself look like the best mate available. This behavior is called **courtship**. Males mostly pay more attention to courtship. Females generally spend more time and energy on laying eggs or giving birth and caring for the young.

Different Ways to Attract Mates

Different types of animals use various ways to attract mates. Some animals display spectacular tail feathers or mighty **antlers** to show that they are strong and healthy. Others bring gifts of food to show that they will be able to feed their young.

Did You Know?

In this book you will find out about:

■ insects that flash bright lights
■ birds that dance and prance
■ spiders that offer gifts
■ fish that stay together for life.

A male great egret displays long, hairlike feathers to show a female that he is healthy.

Greater Sage-grouse

A greater sage-grouse is a chicken-like bird that performs a courtship display on a lek. The lek is a large, open area near sagebrush plants.

In spring, all male greater sage-grouse gather at a few **traditional** leks. Each male chooses and guards a small **territory** in his lek.

The male displays on the lek for several weeks. He sometimes displays for several hours in the morning and again in the evening. He rests after displaying.

Some birds perform courtship displays on shared breeding grounds, known as **leks**.

When females visit, the male struts around the lek. He spreads his tail out until it looks like a spiky fan. He also **inflates** the air sacs on his chest and then deflates them to make popping sounds.

The females watch the display for a few days and then choose the most attractive male to mate with. A few males do most of the mating.

Indian Peafowl

A male Indian peafowl, also called a peacock, displays his beautiful tail feathers to impress a female, called a peahen.

A peacock lifts his tail feathers when a peahen approaches him. The large tail feathers spread out like a fan and reach the ground on both sides. The peacock shakes his tail feathers to make the eyespots on them dance. The feathers make a rustling sound.

Type of Animal: bird

Length: 3 to 9.2 feet (90 cm to 2.8 m)

Habitat: forests

Distribution: Asia

Courtship by: the male

Did You Know?

A peahen chooses the peacock with the most eyespots on his tail. This is because she thinks he will be the strongest mate.

A peacock displays his shimmering blue and green tail feathers to dazzle a peahen.

Did You Know?

A female pin-tailed whydah chooses the male with the longest tail feathers. This is because his long tail shows that he is healthy and has lived for a long time.

Pin-tailed Whydah

A male pin-tailed whydah grows very long, black tail feathers in the breeding season. He displays his tail feathers to attract a female.

Each male pin-tailed whydah guards a territory that has food and nesting bushes in it in the breeding season. The males leap into the air when a female flies past. They do this to show how long and healthy their tail feathers are.

 FACT FILE

Type of Animal: bird

Length: 11.8 to 16.9 inches (30–43 cm)

Habitat: woodlands and grasslands

Distribution: Africa

Courtship by: the male

A male great frigate bird only inflates his red throat pouch in the breeding season.

Did You Know?

A female great frigate bird will join a male at his nest site if she is impressed by his inflated throat pouch.

FACT FILE

Type of Animal: bird

Length: 2.8–3.4 feet (85–105 cm)

Habitat: islands

Distribution: worldwide in warm places

Courtship by: the male

Great Frigate Bird

A male great frigate bird inflates his throat pouch into a huge red balloon so that a female will notice him.

The male great frigate bird chooses a nest site in the breeding season. He stays at the nest site and tries to get the attention of a female. He inflates his throat pouch so that any females flying past will see him. He also shakes his wings, wiggles his head, and makes loud gobbling sounds.

Green Anole

A male green anole displays the pink skin on his throat, called a **dewlap**, to attract a female. He also displays it when defending his territory against other males.

When he sees a female, the male green anole spreads out his dewlap like a fan. He also bobs his head up and down and does "push-ups."

FACT FILE

Type of Animal: reptile

Length: 7.1 inches (18 cm)

Habitat: woodlands

Distribution: North America

Courtship by: the male

Did You Know?

A female green anole allows herself to be caught if she is willing to mate.

The male green anole spreads out his pink dewlap in a courtship display.

Cuttlefish

A male cuttlefish puts on a dazzling color show to attract a female.

In the breeding season, male and female cuttlefish gather in shallow water. The males flash different colors and patterns to impress the females. They also fight with each other, if there are more males than females.

Did You Know?

A female cuttlefish chooses a large male. A small male will sometimes trick a female by changing his colors and patterns to look like a female. He sneaks up to a female and mates with her while the large males are not looking.

A male cuttlefish impresses and wins a female by changing his skin color and pattern.

A firefly has special light organs on the underside of its body, which it uses to find a mate.

FACT FILE

Type of Animal: invertebrate

Length: 0.2–1 inches (5–25 millimeters)

Habitat: wet forests and mangrove swamps

Distribution: every continent except Antarctica

Courtship by: the male

Firefly

A male firefly flashes his light to attract a female. His light is green, yellow, or pale red.

When a male firefly approaches a female firefly, he flashes his light. The female waits for a short period of time and then flashes her light to answer him. The pattern of flashes is different for each type of firefly. This is how a firefly finds a mate of the same type.

A male superb lyrebird sings a beautiful and complex courtship song on top of a mound.

Did You Know?

The song of a male superb lyrebird is full of sounds he has copied, including sounds made by cameras, car alarms, and even chainsaws!

FACT FILE

Type of Animal: bird

Length: 2.6–3.3 feet (80–100 cm)

Habitat: rain forests and forests

Distribution: Australia

Courtship by: the male

Superb Lyrebird

A male lyrebird sings a loud, clear song to persuade females to come closer. His song is a mixture of his own calls and sounds he has heard in the forest.

The male lyrebird builds 10 to 15 mounds of soil at the start of the breeding season. He sings, drapes his tail over his head, and prances on top of the mounds to attract a female. A female superb lyrebird visits a male at his mound if she is impressed by his singing and dancing.

Red Deer

A male red deer roars to attract females in the breeding season. He also roars when **competing** with other males for females and territories.

Male red deer are more active and aggressive in the breeding season, which is known as the **rut**. They size each other up by roaring loudly and walking side by side. Sometimes the males fight each other by locking their antlers together and pushing as hard as they can.

FACT FILE

Type of Animal: mammal

Height at the Shoulder: 3.9 feet (1.2 m)

Habitat: woodlands

Distribution: Africa, Europe, and Asia

Courtship by: the male

Did You Know?

A female red deer chooses the male that has the loudest roar and roars most often, because he is the strongest.

A male red deer sometimes roars for several hours during the rut.

Type of Animal: amphibian

Length: 0.4–11.8 inches
(1–30 cm)

Habitat: rain forests, forests,
swamps, and deserts

Distribution: every continent
except Antarctica

Courtship by: the male

Frog

A male frog calls to attract a female. He calls from a water plant, a tree branch, a drain, or other special place.

Male frogs mostly call during the mating season, especially when it is raining. Each different type of frog has a different call. When a male frog calls, the vocal sac under his mouth swells up and makes his call louder.

Did You Know?

A female frog does not just choose the first male of the same type that she hears. She listens to several males before she makes her choice.

A male frog will sometimes call to a female from a leaf using his swollen vocal sac.

loud mating calls.

A male mole cricket uses his shovel-like front legs to dig a burrow, from which he calls to female mole crickets.

Did You Know?

A female mole cricket will choose a male that calls from a damp burrow because she needs to lay her eggs in a damp place.

Mole Cricket

A male mole cricket makes a very loud call from a burrow to impress females. He usually starts calling at **dusk**.

The male mole cricket digs a specially shaped burrow that makes his call louder. To make the call, he stands at the entrance of the burrow and rubs his wings together very quickly. A call made from a damp burrow sounds different from a call made from a dry burrow.

FACT FILE

Type of Animal: invertebrate

Length: 1.2–1.6 inches (3–4 cm)

Habitat: woodlands and gardens

Distribution: every continent except Antarctica

Courtship by: the male

A male saturniid moth has large **antennae** to help him sense the smell of a female moth.

Did You Know?

A male moth can detect even a tiny amount of a female moth's smell. He can detect the smell from more than 0.6 miles (1 km) away!

FACT FILE

Type of Animal: invertebrate

Length: 0.2–11.8 inches (4–300 mm)

Habitat: forests, woodlands, grasslands, deserts, and swamps

Distribution: every continent except Antarctica

Courtship by: the female

Moth

A female moth releases a special mating smell to attract a male moth. The smell is irresistible to a male moth of the same type.

A male moth senses a female moth's mating smell with his feathery antennae. He follows the smell until he finds the female. The smell helps him find her at nighttime.

Red-sided Garter Snake

A female red-sided garter snake releases a smell that causes her to be surrounded by a **writhing mass of males in seconds.**

Red-sided garter snakes rest in dens in winter. The males come out of the dens first. When a female comes out of a den, she releases a smell to tell the males that she is ready to mate. The males slither all over her, forming a huge ball, called a mating ball.

FACT FILE

Type of Animal: reptile

Length: 15.7–26 inches (40–66 cm)

Habitat: forests, grasslands, and wetlands

Distribution: North America

Courtship by: the female

Did You Know?

A male red-sided garter snake sometimes releases a female smell to make the other males surround him. Then he sneaks away and mates with the nearest female!

A female red-sided garter snake releases a smell that can attract more than 100 males.

Blue-footed Booby

A male blue-footed booby does a high-stepping courtship dance. The dance shows off his bright blue feet.

When he is interested in a female, a male spreads his wings, lifts his tail, and points his beak toward the sky. Then he walks around the female with high steps that draw attention to his blue feet. The female points her beak towards the sky if she likes him.

Did You Know?

A female blue-footed booby chooses a male with large blue feet. This is because both parents need to keep the eggs warm with their feet.

A male blue-footed booby lifts one blue foot, then the other, during his courtship dance.

Red-crowned cranes leap into the air with their legs dangling beneath them during their courtship dance.

Did You Know?

Red-crowned cranes usually mate for life. They use a special call, known as a unison call, to cry out to each other and further strengthen their relationship.

Red-crowned Crane

Red-crowned cranes are known for their spectacular courtship dance. The dance helps strengthen the relationship between a male and a female.

A male and a female red-crowned crane dance with each other to show that they are a pair. They bow to each other and leap high into the air, before prancing around each other with their wings flapping. They often toss sticks or grass into the air.

 FACT FILE

Type of Animal: bird

Height: 4.9 feet (1.5 m)

Habitat: marshlands, wet meadows, and rivers

Distribution: Asia

Courtship by: the male and female

White-tailed sea eagles sometimes roll in the air with their feet locked during a courtship flight.

Did You Know?

A female eagle will choose a male if he shows her that he is a very good flyer.

FACT FILE

Type of Animal: bird

Length: 18.9–39.4 inches (48–100 cm)

Habitat: forests, woodlands, and grasslands

Distribution: every continent except Antarctica

Courtship by: the male

Eagle

A male eagle flies above a nest site to impress a female. He flies to a great height and then dives down at breathtaking speed.

A male eagle flies in circles up into the sky until he can barely be seen, before diving down with his wings folded back. Sometimes the female joins the male in the sky. If he dives towards her, she rolls onto her back as he approaches.

Butterfly

A male butterfly flies near a female he wants to mate with in order to display his colorful wings.

The male butterfly flies around or sits on a plant while he is looking for a female at breeding time. He recognizes a female of the same type by the colors and patterns on her wings. He flies around her and releases a special mating smell from scales on his front wings.

FACT FILE

Type of Animal: invertebrate

Length: 0.5–11.8 inches (12–300 mm)

Habitat: rain forests, forests, woodlands, grasslands, mangrove swamps, and deserts

Distribution: every continent except Antarctica

Courtship by: the male

Did You Know?

A female butterfly chooses a male if she senses his mating smell. She only mates with a male if she has not already mated.

A male butterfly (top) flutters his wings more than usual when he is courting a female.

Satin Bowerbird

A male satin bowerbird builds a structure called a **bower** to impress females. He decorates the bower with blue objects that he collects.

The male satin bowerbird builds his bower in the shape of a long avenue with two walls made of sticks. He decorates the platforms at each end with blue objects, such as flowers, berries, and sticks. When a female arrives, he prances and struts around his bower.

FACT FILE

Type of Animal: bird

Length: 10.6–13 inches (27–33 cm)

Habitat: rain forests, forests, and woodlands

Distribution: Australia

Courtship by: the male

Did You Know?

A female satin bowerbird mates with a male if she is impressed with his bower and his blue objects.

A male satin bowerbird (right) often brings blue feathers back to his bower.

A male brown gardener's bower is often as large as a child's playhouse.

Did You Know?

A female brown gardener chooses a male if she likes his bower and his treasures.

Brown Gardener

A male brown gardener builds a huge bower to attract females. He arranges colored objects in and around the bower.

The male builds his bower in the shape of a large hut made of sticks. He clears the ground in front of the bower and plants a "lawn" of moss. He collects treasures, such as flowers, berries, and leaves, and arranges them in neat piles on the moss. He keeps these treasures in good condition to impress passing females.

FACT FILE

Type of Animal: bird

Length: 9.8 inches (25 cm)

Habitat: rain forests

Distribution: Indonesia

Courtship by: the male

A male nursery web spider carrying a gift of food (left) has a better chance of mating with a female (right).

Did You Know?

A hungry female nursery web spider is more likely to accept a gift of food and allow a male to mate with her.

FACT FILE

Type of Animal: invertebrate

Length: 0.4–0.6 inches (10–15 mm)

Habitat: woodlands

Distribution: Europe

Courtship by: the male

Nursery Web Spider

A male nursery web spider offers a gift of food to a female at mating time. He mates with the female while she is busy eating the food.

The male spider approaches a female very carefully, because she might mistake him for prey and gobble him up. He holds out a gift of food, such as a caterpillar, or he sometimes plays dead, with the gift of food in his mouth. When the female takes the gift, he "comes to life" and mates with her.

Tern

A male tern brings a female a gift of fish when he wants to mate with her. He puts the fish into her beak.

The male tern catches a fish by diving headfirst into the sea. He sometimes flies above the female with the fish held in his beak, then he lands on the ground and offers her the fish. He sometimes parades around with his shoulders down and his neck stretched up.

FACT FILE

Type of Animal: bird

Length: 7.9–21.7 inches (20–55 cm)

Habitat: coasts, lagoons, and rivers

Distribution: worldwide

Courtship by: the male

Did You Know?

A female tern chooses a male that gives her food. This is because she needs a mate that will bring her food when she is sitting on the eggs.

A male Arctic tern passes his gift of a fish to a female while she is on the ground.

A male southern elephant seal fights other males for mating rights. He is sometimes badly injured during these fights.

Male southern elephant seals become very aggressive during the breeding season. A male fights with other males to defend his territory and for the right to mate with the females. He pushes other males and strikes them with his teeth and his trunk. The male also roars loudly to further threaten other males.

Did You Know?

A female southern elephant seal chooses the male that is the best fighter. She shares him with up to 50 other females.

Male southern elephant seals often have scars on their necks from fighting over females.

Male moose fight and mate for several weeks during the rut.

Did You Know?

The male moose that wins a pushing fight with another male usually gets to mate with the female.

Moose

A male moose fights fiercely for females during the rut. He tries to gore males of a similar size with his huge antlers.

The male finds a female by following her call and her smell. He leaves her alone if a larger male is nearby. If a male of similar size is nearby, he displays his antlers. The two males bring their antlers together and try to push each other away.

FACT FILE

Type of animal: mammal

Height at Shoulder: 4.9–6.6 feet (1.5–2 m)

Habitat: forests

Distribution: Europe, Asia, and North America

Courtship by: the male

Staying Together

A female deep-sea anglerfish may have one or two males **permanently** attached to her body.

Did You Know?

A male deep-sea anglerfish has large eyes to help him find a female in the deep ocean. He also has a white organ in front of his eyes that is used for sensing a smell released by the female.

FACT FILE

Type of Animal: fish

Length: up to 3.9 feet (1.2 m)

Habitat: the deep ocean

Distribution: worldwide in all oceans

Courtship by: the female

Deep-sea Anglerfish

A female deep-sea anglerfish flashes a light and releases a smell to attract mates. When a male finds her, he permanently attaches himself to her!

The male deep-sea anglerfish bites into the belly of a female when he finds her. He becomes joined to her and her body takes control of his. This means that the male is always there when the female is ready to release eggs.

amphibian	an animal that spends the first part of its life living in water and the second part of its life living on land
antennae	structures on the heads of insects and some other animals
antlers	structures on the heads of members of the deer family
bower	a structure built by a male, used to attract females
breeding	having young
competing	trying to do better than one or more others in order to win something
courtship	special behaviors carried out to attract a mate
dewlap	a flap of skin on the throat
dusk	the time of evening when it is half light and half dark
gore	to make a hole using horns or tusks
inflates	blows up
invertebrate	an animal without a backbone
irresistible	so tempting that an animal cannot resist or ignore it
leks	shared breeding grounds
mammal	an animal that feeds its young with its own milk
permanently	lasting forever
predators	animals that hunt and kill other animals for food
reptile	a creeping or crawling animal that is covered with scales
rut	the breeding season of members of the deer family
territory	an area occupied by an animal, a mating pair of animals, or a group of animals
traditional	something that has been done in the same way for a very long time
writhing	twisting the body

A

Africa 9, 15
American alligators 4
amphibians 16
Asia 8, 15, 21, 29
Atlantic Ocean 28
Australia 14, 24

B

birds 6–7, 8, 9, 10, 14, 20, 21, 22, 24, 25, 27
blue-footed boobies 20
brown gardeners 25
building 14, 24–5
butterflies 23

C

calling 14, 16–17, 21, 29
colors 10–11, 12–13, 23, 24, 25
courtship by females 18, 19, 21, 30
courtship by males 6–7, 8, 9, 10, 11, 12, 13, 14, 15, 16, 17, 20, 21, 22, 23, 24, 25, 26, 27, 28, 29
cuttlefish 12

D

dancing 5, 8, 14, 20–21
deep-sea anglerfish 30
displaying 5, 6–7, 8–9, 11, 23, 29

E

eagles 22
Europe 15, 26, 29

F

fighting 15, 28–9
fireflies 13
fish 5, 27, 30
flying 10, 22–3
frogs 16

G

Galapagos Islands 20
giving gifts 5, 26–7
great egrets 5
greater sage-grouse 6–7
great frigate birds 10
green anoles 11

I

Indian peafowls 8
Indonesia 25
invertebrates 12, 13, 17, 18, 23, 26

L

lights 13

M

mammals 15, 28, 29
mole crickets 17
moose 29
moths 18

N

North America 11, 19, 20, 29
nursery web spiders 26

P

peacocks 8
pin-tailed whydahs 9

R

red-crowned cranes 21
red deer 15
red-sided garter snakes 19
reptiles 11, 19

S

satin bowerbirds 24
smells 18–19, 23, 29, 30
songs 14
sounds 6–7, 8, 10, 14–15, 16–17, 21, 28, 29
South America 20
southern elephant seals 28
Southern Ocean 28
sub-Antarctic islands 28
superb lyrebirds 14

T

tails 5, 6–7, 8–9, 14, 20
tern 27
territory 6–7, 9, 11, 15, 28